RHÉO 8

(

RHÉO & MICHELLE COURCHESNE
C.P. 222
193, Rue Main Nord
Callander, Ontario P0H 1H0

FIFTY USEFUL HERBS

FIFTY USEFUL **HERBS**

ANTHONY GARDINER

PRC

This edition published 1996 by
Promotional Reprint Company Ltd
Kiln House, 210 New Kings Road
London SW6 4NZ
for Chapters in Canada

ISBN 1 85648 382 7

ACKNOWLEDGEMENTS

The publishers wish to thank Simon Hopkinson of Hollington Nurseries for his invaluable help in providing the herbs for photography.

Printed and bound in China

CONTENTS

Now it behoves anyone, who desires to be a skilful herbalist, to be present when the plants first shoot out of the earth, when they are fully grown, and when they begin to fade. For he who is only present at the budding of the herb, cannot know it when full-grown, nor can he who hath examined a full-grown herb, recognise it when it has only just appeared above ground.

Dioscorides, AD 60

THE HERBS

Achillea millefolium

Yarrow

Family: Compositae
Other names: Soldier's woundwort, *herbe militaris*, nose bleed, carpenter's weed, yarroway
Life: Perennial

The finely divided grey-green leaves of yarrow led William Coles, in his *Doctrine of Signatures*, to believe that this was a herb which should help in blood disorders, because of the appearance of the leaf, which resembles a network of veins. Although William Coles' theory has now been discredited, yarrow has always had a reputation as a styptic, and today is used by medical herbalists to dissolve clots in thrombosis, for the treatment of varicose veins and piles. I once cut myself quite badly with a pair of secateurs and, with no sticking plaster in sight, wrapped the wound with yarrow leaves. Crushed, to release the oil, and applied, tied about with twine, I was amazed at the speed with which the flow of blood was stemmed and the wound healed perfectly. Evidence of the antiseptic quality was clear, as I failed to get any infection in the soil-covered cut. Perhaps I was lucky, but it certainly led me to believe in the legend of Achilles healing his soldiers' wounds on the field of battle with yarrow. Its name derives from this ancient hero and the word 'milfoil', meaning 'thousand-leafed'. Yarrow staunches nose bleeds, but also promotes them if rubbed in the nostrils. It was used as a cure for headache; also a masochistic 'love charm' if the old East Anglian rhyme is to be taken seriously: 'Yarroway, Yarroway, bear a white blow,/If my love love me, my nose will bleed now.'

I grow yarrow mostly for its ability to inhabit rough places, although the flat heads of tiny white flowers are attractive, even though the herb has a straggly appearance. As a flu and cold tonic, yarrow, elderflower and peppermint in equal parts, taken every two hours, takes away much of the discomfort.

Alchemilla vulgaris

Lady's Mantle

Family: Rosaceae
Other names: Lion's foot, bear's foot, nine hooks, Stellaria
Life: Perennial

Lady's mantle is one of nature's 'magic' herbs, dedicated to Mary, mother of Jesus, by the early Christians. Its name, however, derives from the Arabic word 'alkemelych' meaning alchemy. It was recognised from very early times as a wondrous healer, and it is easy to appreciate the reverence with which it was kept when you see, early in the morning sun, the tiny spherical droplets of dew on its cloak-shaped leaves. This is as good a reason as any to include it in your herb garden, but I have grown borders of this graceful plant more for its frothy yellow flowers, which stand only 30cm/12in above the soft green leaves. It increases each season so be careful to divide the roots either in spring or late autumn so that it does not become overcrowded. It will also self-seed freely. In the wild it is often found in shady woodlands, but it will grow well in full sun too.

Medicinally, lady's mantle is classed as a 'woman's' herb. It has been used most effectively to strengthen the womb and is therefore considered by medical herbalists to be a good tonic to aid in conception. It has also been used in the treatment of painful periods, and before and after childbirth. The gentle visual look of this beautiful herb seems to suggest its caring qualities. Traditionally it was used as a 'wound' herb.

Lady's mantle is a favourite with flower arrangers as it makes a soft contrast to strong leaf forms. The dwarf form, *Alchemilla alpina,* makes a very pretty addition to a small sink or trough.

Although I look upon this herb as a safe herb, I would never advise self-medication in cases of pregnancy. Always consult a registered medical herbalist or doctor who will prescribe a carefully formulated tincture and monitor your progress.

Allium schoenoprasum

Chives

Family: Liliaceae
Other names: Rushe onyons, rush leeks, chibal
Life: Perennial

Chives are known as 'the little brothers of the onion'. They are among the first herbs to show after the winter, pushing their bright green spear-like leaves up from the ground. This is the best time to lift and divide them in order to increase your crop. By dividing the tiny bulblets into clusters of between 8 and 10 you can create a border for the summer. If allowed to flower the stems support globular mauve heads of closely-packed umbels. If you are using chives for culinary purposes it is best to remove the flowers as they create thick woody stems that are inedible, and this also tends to weaken the rest of the plant.

The cylindrical leaves grow to a height of about 25cm/10in and should be cut lightly on a regular basis. This ensures a continual crop throughout the year and helps to avoid yellowing-off at the tips. I find chives grow well in light shade with plenty of moisture. This is one herb that doesn't mind getting its feet wet, and can therefore be grown very effectively near sources of fresh water.

The Romans introduced chives into the British Isles; the herb's other common English name, 'Rush leeks', is the English translation of the Latin name. The mild onion flavour helps to make it a wonderful addition to summer salads. Dried and crushed with a coarse sea salt it makes a chive salt which can be stored in jars. As a member of the garlic family it has a reputation for being a good blood tonic; it is also a safe and useful convalescent herb for children.

The flat-leafed variety known as Chinese or garlic chives has very pretty white flowers similar to wild garlic. Divide large chive clumps every year, otherwise the plant becomes coarse and loses its strong volatile oils, which are so essential to its flavour.

Angelica archangelica

Angelica

Family: Umbelliferae
Other names: Holy ghost root, masterwort
Life: Biennial

A truly architectural plant, angelica can grow to a height of 2m/ 6½ ft, displaying large umbels of flowers very attractive to bees. I have also found it, sadly, susceptible to blackfly, so keep a close watch for this problem. It can be sown in autumn or divided, and is best planted in rich, well-drained soil allowing for the possibility of light shade. In less sheltered positions its thick stems and stalks may need to be staked. If allowed to flower it dies off quite quickly, so you should regularly clip flower heads if you wish it to take on a perennial nature.

Angelica has a strong tradition as a protective herb against evil and witchcraft. It was, therefore, associated with the archangel Michael, slayer of dragons. This was chiefly because of the fact that it flowers at about the same time as the old festival of St Michael (8 May) and was said to be a powerful remedy against the Great Plague which devastated London in 1665.

Used today more as a flavouring (its stems can be candied) and decoration, it is reputed to be a secret ingredient in the liqueur chartreuse. Research has shown this herb to be rich in medicinal properties, giving relief to indigestion, anaemia, coughs, and colds. It is antibacterial, anti-fungal, a diuretic and an expectorant as well as acting as a stimulant to the circulation. It also induces sweating and has an anti-spasmodic action which helps in treating painful periods. However, in some people it can cause photosensitivity, so although it may appear to be one of nature's 'cure-alls' care should be taken in its medicinal use.

The famous English herbalist Nicholas Culpeper wrote of this herb: 'Some call this an Herb of the Holy Ghost, others more moderate call it Angelica because of its' Angelic Vertues.'

Anthemis nobilis

Chamomile

Family: Compositae
Other names: Roman chamomile, maythen, ground apple
Life: Perennial

If you wish to plant a chamomile seat, *Anthemis nobilis* is the low-growing variety to use. It is a herb that likes to be trodden or sat upon. In recent years, a sterile carpeting variety called 'Treneague' has been developed and this is ideal for using in the making of lawns. Do not, however, be tempted to cover vast tracts with this sweet-smelling herb. The area needs careful weeding beforehand and the ideal size is no more than 6sq m/ 64sq ft.

Although clipping is confined to once or twice in the summer, the chamomile lawn or seat is labour intensive in its upkeep, requiring constant vigilance for weeds and gaps – created by its creeping nature – to be filled. However there is no more fragrant and restful place to sit than on a sunny cultivated lawn or bench of chamomile. This most comforting herb has been loved by gardeners and medical herbalists alike for centuries. It makes a soothing, flavoursome tea and an excellent calming syrup for recalcitrant children. Frances A Bardsweel, in *The Herb Garden* (1911), writes about chamomile that, 'It will revive drooping and sickly plants if placed near them.'

A raised bed of the double flowering *Anthemis nobilis* 'Flore pleno' was a favourite bed for a visiting vixen to my previous nursery. This somewhat negated the smell of the chamomile, but provided a sanctuary for this useful animal. While she was around I had no trouble from rats or mice. Neither was there any animosity between her and the cats.

There is a wild woodland form of chamomile called Mayweed, or 'stinking chamomile'. This has a foetid smell, which distinguishes it from others. The German chamomile, *A. matricaria*, is an annual and grows much taller than the perennial.

Anethum graveolens

Dill

Family: Umbelliferae
Other names: Dillseed, dillweed, anetum
Life: Annual

I have long since given up growing dill in small pots for selling on. It is not fair to the plant and it is not fair to the customer. Dill does not take kindly to transplanting and goes to flower very quickly as a protest. Since you tend to grow dill for its delicate, feathery leaf then a wiser strategy is to purchase a good seed, such as Dukat, and grow in situ.

Dill needs a light soil in a sunny position protected from winds. It grows to a height of 50-90cm/24-36in. The leaves are blue-grey in colour and the dark green stalks bear four umbels of yellow florets. Sow in the spring and then sow successively for two more months. Avoid growing it anywhere near fennel as the two plants cross-pollinate easily. Dill is also known to have an adverse effect on carrots and tomatoes.

The name originates from the old Norse word 'dilla', meaning 'to lull'. This may account for its use for many years as an ingredient of gripe water, used as a remedy for colic in babies.

Dill is used especially in the pickling of cucumbers, and is also mainly associated with a sauce for fish and as a flavouring for bland vegetables. Its reputation for stimulating the appetite, as well as assuaging hunger, gave it the name 'meeting house', as during the 17th and 18th centuries the seeds were chewed to alleviate the boredom that occurred during long dry sermons.

The only related species is *Anethum sowa*, known as Indian, or Japanese, dill, which is used as an ingredient in Asian cooking.

The medieval health handbook *Tacuinum Sanitatus* (c1345) includes the following comment on dill: 'Brings relief to a stomach that is cold and windy.'

Anthriscus cerefolium

Chervil

Family: Umbelliferae
Other names: Salad chervil, beaked parsley
Life: Annual

In many ways chervil resembles parsley to look at, but on closer examination you will be able to see that its foliage is more feathery and fernlike. Like chamomile, a lover of well-drained soil, it will grow in most types of soil but prefers a light shade. This can be easily achieved by planting it beneath taller herbs or vegetables. It is a herb that will grow right through the winter months and as such is a very good complementary herb in cooking. It is for this very reason that it is a prime ingredient of the culinary herbs known as *fines herbes*.

If chervil is sown in the cooling days of late summer it can provide two harvests before the end of winter, and early in the following year you can begin successive sowing every month. When harvesting, you should treat it in a similar way to parsley by taking a leaf from the outside. Chervil goes into flower very quickly and then tends to lose its flavour, so cut off the flower heads before they open. By cutting the plant down to the ground you can assure another crop.

This is not a difficult herb to grow provided you keep it cool and moist. If you are growing from seed, germination will take up to a maximum of six weeks. The seed should always be sown in situ. Transplanted seedlings tend to 'bolt' (run to seed) rather quickly.

Chervil is a culinary herb of great importance to chefs and cooks as a prime ingredient for Béarnaise sauce. It also makes a marvellous soup. It can be added to meat, fish, poultry and game as well as omelettes and salads. It is extremely versatile.

John Parkinson, in *Paradisus* (1629) writes of its use as a culinary herb: 'Sweet Chervil is so like in taste unto Anis seede that it much delighteth the taste among other herbs in a sallet.'

Artemisia abrotanum

Southernwood

Family: Compositae
Other names: Lad's love, old man, maiden's ruin, garde-robe
Life: Perennial

The feathery grey-green leaves of this decorative, aromatic shrub have been used in many ways over the centuries. It was called 'lad's love' because young boys would give a sprig of it to their girlfriends at church on Sundays. Placed in a nosegay, it also helped to sweeten the air in the often crowded congregations. The name 'old man' came about because of the grey, old beard effect it gives at the end of the season. Young boys used to rub their faces with it to promote a beard. The French gave it the name *'garde-robe'* when they used it to hang in wardrobes to deter the moth. I find it most effective for this purpose.

'Maiden's ruin' comes from the belief that it was a love charm and aphrodisiac. It has been used to treat female ailments for centuries. The leaves and flowering tops have been used to treat delayed menstruation, threadworms in children and diseases of the scalp. This herb prefers a gritty, well drained soil in full sun, growing to a height and spread of 1m/39in. At the start of the growing season in early spring, cut back to new shoots about 30cm/12in above the ground. It will shape into a nice hedge if you trim it in early summer. Cut off the yellow flower heads. Cuttings take well in the summer and can be overwintered in the greenhouse until the spring. It looks particularly good when planted with lavender and rosemary.

There are several varieties of artemisia, but the one most similar in look to southernwood is *Artemisia camphorata*. Like southernwood, it does not produce anything much in the way of flower, but the scent is quite different, being a heady, sweet smell of camphor, which some people find very pleasant. It makes a good herb for gardens planted especially for the blind.

Artemisia absinthium

Wormwood

Family: Compositae
Other names: Green ginger, absinth, St John's girdle
Life: Perennial

Taking its name from its ability to expel worms, this aromatic, silver-leafed herb is a powerful bitter. Wormwood was introduced into this country in 1548 and became a 'monastic' herb, probably as a result of the legend that St John the Baptist wore a girdle of wormwood around his waist. It is not, however, accepted that the wormwood we know today is that which is mentioned in the bible. Traditionally, it was looked upon as a herb for women's ailments and classed with the other artemisias. It was used to promote menstruation, and as a tonic before and after childbirth. Today, its ability to restore the appetite has meant that it has been used in cases of anorexia nervosa. But it has a down side too. Its bitter principle is absinthum, which went into the flavouring of the French drink, absinthe. This was found to be addictive and to have a destructive effect on the central nervous system, in severe cases causing epileptic fits. Taken as a tea it can have quite alarming hallucinogenic properties, as indeed its sister plant, 'mugwort' (*Artemisia vulgaris*), also has. Treated with respect and taken in small doses, wormwood is an excellent digestive bitter tonic, but I would always advise seeking qualified medical help before attempting any kind of self treatment with this herb.

I find it grows well in the garden in sun, or shade, although it prefers a shady position. As it grows to a height of 1.2m/4ft, it should be placed towards the back of a border. The small clusters of yellow flowers in late summer are insignificant. It is best propagated by root division, in spring, otherwise take softwood cuttings in early summer. Dried, it makes a good moth repellent and you can infuse it for use as an insecticide. It is not a good companion to roses.

Artemisia dracunculus

Tarragon

Family: Compositae
Other names: Little dragon, *herbe au dragon*
Life: Perennial

The major difference between this French tarragon and coarser Russian tarragon, *Artemisia redowski* (sometimes listed as *A. dracunculoides*), is in the form of propagation. French tarragon is a sterile plant, which, although it goes to flower, rarely sets seed. It is propagated by root division in spring or autumn, or by soft-wood cuttings in the summer. The roots have a similar pattern to mint and it is advisable to contain them by use of roof slates, or by placing them in a sunken container with the base removed. I find it grows best in poor, stony soil with plenty of sun. Having died down in the winter it should surface again in the spring if it has had some protection from hard frosts. A good late mulch is beneficial, or you can dig it up and bring it inside for the winter. It grows to a height of 1m/39in, with woody, branching stems producing an abundance of dark green, pointed leaves. To harvest the leaves, it is best to do so before flowers appear around about midsummer. They should be cut very carefully so as not to bruise the leaves, which makes them lose their flavour. Dry in a dark, cool place, and use to make vinegar. Although it is a very versatile herb it is mainly used in salads and with chicken dishes. It is also the main ingredient in tartare sauce.

Although not introduced into this country until Tudor times, it was well known as a cure for toothache by the Arabs. Its name derives from the Latin, '*dracunculus*', meaning 'little dragon', as it had a reputation for curing stings and bites from venomous reptiles.

Do try to avoid this herb's larger cousin, Russian tarragon, which grows into a large and unruly bush, producing seed in abundance and yet having very little flavour.

Balsamita major tanacetiodes

Costmary

Family: Compositae
Other names: Alecost, balsamita, balsam herb, maudlin
Life: Perennial

Costmary, or alecost, can grow up to 45cm/18in high. The leaves are finely toothed, entire in shape and have a delightful balsam scent. This herb was used in medieval times for flavouring beer, from which it derives its name. I was first encouraged to grow costmary having learned of its use as a bookmark for bibles. It acts as a sweet antidote to musty-smelling books, the scent lasting for many months, with the herb taking on a paper-thin translucent quality when dried between the pages. The tiny clusters of yellow flowers in late summer are insignificant.

Costmary will grow in almost any soil and can be divided in the spring or autumn; it should be placed at least 60cm/24in apart to allow it sufficient room to spread. I have found it unable to cope with hindrance from other plants which grow in close proximity.

In France it is known as *herbe Sainte-Marie* and is dedicated to Mary Magdalene, giving rise to the country name of 'maudlin'. It is said to help clear catarrh when taken as a tisane and has been used as both a strewing herb and as a tasteful and aromatic addition to green salads.

Camphor is a similar plant which looks strikingly like costmary. The herb's botanical name is *Balsamita vulgaris* 'Tomentosum', and it grows to a height of 1m/39in. It has white daisy-like flowers and the foliage smells strongly of camphor. There is also a golden variety called *Tanacetum parthenium aureum*, which has white flowers and grows to a height of 45cm/18in.

Nicholas Culpeper summed up costmary's beneficial qualities in the following manner: 'It is an especial friend to evil, weak and cold livers.'

Borago officinalis

Borage

Family: Boraginaceae
Other names: Beebread, starflower burrage, bugloss
Life: Annual

The beautiful, bright blue star-shaped flowers of borage cheer the eye as much as the stems and fresh young leaves reputably cheer the heart. Once you have borage in your garden you should have it for life as it self-seeds freely. If sown in early spring in a sunny, well-drained soil you should have flowers by July.

If you are very lucky the flowers will appear in early summer, die off and self-seed to produce more flowers during the early autumn. It does not take too kindly to transplanting, so it is advisable to sow in situ or in small pots. Borage is best displayed on a slope where the flowers can hang down, and therefore it makes a good rockery plant.

Borage grows to a height of 60-90cm/2-3ft and has thick hairy stems with rough leaves. Hairs on the underside of the leaves will sting when touched, so be careful when handling it. The herb loses this quality when placed into cordial drinks, flavouring them faintly with just a hint of cucumber. Flowers that have been placed into an ice cube tray make a very attractive addition to summer cocktails and cordials.

Medical research has shown that the early herbalists were right to recognise the uplifting qualities of borage. It contains high levels of gamma linoleic acid, useful in many disorders and an aid to blood clotting. It appears to have a stimulating effect on the adrenal glands. This could substantiate the theory that the leaves and seeds help to increase the milk in nursing mothers. As an infusion it has been used for colds and flu. John Gerard, in *The Herbal* (1597), says of borage: 'Pliny calleth it Euphrosinum, because it makes a man merry and joyfull: which thing also the old verse concerning Borage doth testifie: "I Borage bring alwaies courage".'

Calendula officinalis

Pot Marigold

Family: Compositae
Other names: Pot marigold, calendula, golds, ruddes
Life: Annual

Pot marigold is a favourite of cottage gardens, primarily because of its colour, but also because it grows easily and rewards the gardener with flowers throughout the summer months and well into the autumn.

Sown in a light soil and thinned out to at least 45cm/18in apart, marigolds make a lovely border. As the flowers die off you should dead-head them so that more will appear. The orange or yellow flowers grow on single stems; the petals can be used to decorate salads most effectively.

Pot marigold has always been associated with the sun, and Charles I of England is reputed to have said: 'The marigold observes the Sun/More than my subjects me have done.'

Pot marigold is a great natural healing plant, a warm, friendly herb with soft hairy leaves and resinous feel. It has anti-inflammatory, antiseptic, anti-fungal actions, which makes it an excellent 'wound' herb, good for oral thrush, throat infections, leg ulcers, excema, mouth ulcers, inflammation of the middle ear and for clearing the fallopian tubes. It also relaxes spasms and generally cheers the heart.

Historically, marigold also has a dark side: it is associated with jealousy, probably because of its resemblance to the emblematic shields worn on the left arm of fighters in Provence. There the marigold is called *gauchefer*, and Chaucer refers to the flowers being worn as a jealous garland. Marigolds derive the name *calendula* from the Greek word 'kalends', referring to the first days of the month when the plant was reputed to be in flower. Its virtues are considerable and it self-seeds freely, assuring a good crop the following year. In fact the self-sown marigolds flower early.

Chenopodium bonus-henricus

Good King Henry

Family: Chenopodiaceae
Other names: English mercury, fat hen, poor man's asparagus, goose foot, smearwort
Life: Perennial

An early-growing spinach substitute, good king henry thrives on a deeply dug, well cultivated soil in partial shade or full sun. French legend would have us believe that the name was derived from a decree by Henry IV of France that all peasants should have a weekly fowl to eat. This chicken was fattened and stewed with the herb, and this would help to explain its country name 'fat hen'. Because of this kindly action, Henry IV is still thought of with affection by the working people of France.

After the first year, cut the leaves on a regular basis to encourage the plant to regenerate. It is best grown from seed in spring, in situ, and doesn't like being transplanted. In summer it produces tiny clusters of pale yellow flowers on coarse stems. These should be cut off to ensure a plentiful supply of leaf. Traditionally, good king henry has been used for poultices to treat sores, and the leaves were used to aid digestion. The leaves resemble a goose's foot, a fact reflected in both the English name 'goosefoot', and in the Latin name *chenopodium*, derived from the Greek for 'goose foot'.

Two closely related species are common orache, or iron root, *Atriplex patula*, and American wormseed, *C. ambrosiodes*. Common orache is native to Britain, where it grows on wasteground: American wormseed is native to tropical regions of America, from where it was introduced into Europe. Like good king henry, this plant has medicinal uses. It has antispasmodic qualities and has been found to be useful in the treatment of asthma, nervous ailments and menstrual disorders. It is also known to expel worms living in the intestine. However, this herb should only be used under medical supervision.

Coriandrum sativum

Coriander

Family: Umbelliferae
Other names: Cilantro
Life: Annual

Coriander is a herb with worldwide popularity. Pliny claimed the best to be from Egypt, where it was used extensively as a medicinal plant. Seeds of coriander were found in Tutankhamun's tomb. Maude Grieve, in her *Modern Herbal* (1931), tells us that in Peru it is so much liked that it 'enters into almost all their dishes'. Anyone who has been to an Asian market knows of the enormous bunches to be had there.

If your climate is dry and hot then this is an easy herb to grow. If you are likely to suffer a wet, cold period in summer then don't be disappointed if you have crop failure. Sow once there is no fear of frosts and thin out seedlings to about 15cm/6in, allowing for the fact that the feathery leaves need support. Dill is a good companion plant and can offer the support needed. Either that or grow in full rows or clumps. The soil should be well-drained and sunny. Successive sowing is best as it goes to seed quickly. Forms such as coriander 'Cilantro' that put all their energies into producing leaf are available, but even these are prone to bolt eventually. The ball-like seeds, however, are important for culinary use, and maintain their flavour for a long time. Coriander has been used for many years as a digestive herb and for the relief of flatulence.

Pliny also recommended its use as an antidote for the 'poison of the two-headed serpent', also with honey and raisins to heal spreading sores, for diseased testes, burns, carbuncles, sore ears and fluxes of the eyes. He suggests making a drink of coriander and rue for cholera and using the seed for expelling intestinal parasites, all of which demonstrates the fact that this is not a good subject for conversation before breakfast.

Digitalis purpurea

Foxglove

Family: Scrophulariaceae
Other names: Bloody fingers, dead men's bells. Virgin's glove, fairy thimbles, fairy caps
Life: Biennial

The large number of different varieties of modern foxglove make this a must for any herb garden, in spite of the fact that every part of it is poisonous. It is amazing to think that not many deaths were recorded from the use of digitalis before the discovery by Doctor William Withering, in the late 18th century, of its stimulating effect on the heart. Today, the heart drug digitoxin is produced from *Digitalis purpurea*. This is such a powerful herb that it should only be used under the guidance of a qualified medical herbalist or doctor.

Foxglove is tremendously attractive to bees. The flowers do not appear until the second year, when they rise on long spikes from a rosette of thick, downy leaves. John Gerard describes them as 'set in a course one by another upon one side of the stalke, hanging downwards with the bottome upward, in forme long, like almost to finger stalkes, whereof it tooke his name "*Digitalis*".'

It is worth noting that although bees and other insects visit the foxglove and use it for shelter on wet, cold days, other animals, by instinct, do not graze on foxgloves. Our fox never went near them, so proving the corruption of the word from 'folksglove'. The only legend that points to the fox comes from Norway, where the bad fairies were supposed to cover the fox's paws with the flowers in order to soften the sound of his tread.

Two varieties worth considering are the woody foxglove *D. lanata*, which has white flowers, and the yellow-flowered foxglove *D. lutea*. They are both only 50cm/18in in height. *D. purpurea* can grow to a height of 2m/6ft. Ideal conditions are a hot, sunny, well-drained bank protected by trees. It thrives when given plenty of leaf mould.

Filipendula ulmaria

Meadowsweet

Family: Rosaceae
Other names: Queen of the meadows, meadwort, meadsweet, dollof, bridewort
Life: Perennial

Meadowsweet is often referred to as 'nature's aspirin'. This is because it contains salicylic acid in its flowerbuds and it is this constituent that was isolated from the plant and made into the drug we know today as 'aspirin'. This name comes from the herb's old botanical name *Spirea ulmaria*. What is interesting to note is that while aspirin causes the stomach lining to bleed, if meadowsweet is used the other constituents of the plant help to relieve stomach acidity. This is probably one of the best examples of holistic medicine that traditional methods can show.

Meadowsweet flowers have a delightful vanilla scent and make a most pleasant drink at night. It has been shown to have an anti-depressant effect.

In the wild it grows in shady areas by streams and on moist banks, and when in flower has a fluffy cloud-like appearance. It is 1.25m/4ft in height with reddish stems and decorative pinnate leaves. The frothy flowers appear in mid to late summer. Plant it where it will get plenty of moisture, in full sun or partial shade. Seed is best sown in situ and it can be propagated by root division in the spring. The herb was often used as a strewing herb, and was made into mead sweetened with honey. It was also used as a flavouring in beer.

Meadowsweet was a sacred herb of the Druids. Elizabeth I gave it her royal blessing, creating a post for women who were especially trained to carry baskets of meadowsweet in front of her at ceremonials, and to broadcast the flowers before her.

Related species are *F. ulmaria* 'Variegata' with gold-splashed foliage, and *F. ulmaria* 'Aurea' with bright gold foliage. They all have cream flowers.

Foeniculum vulgare

Fennel

Family: Umbelliferae
Other names: Finkle, fenkle, sweet fennel, wild fennel
Life: Perennial

Fennel, with its tall fronds of green feathery leaves, looks splendid at the back of a border. I particularly like the bronze form standing in front of a golden hop. The flowers grow in yellow umbels, allowing the plant to grow up to a height of 2m/6ft. For a continual supply of leaf through the summer it is best to keep cutting the plant down to prevent it going to seed. It is not a very good companion herb for coriander and should not be grown near dill as it is likely to cross-fertilise. The old saying 'Fennel for your kennel' originated from its reputation as a flea repellent, but could well have suggested that this is also an ideal way to keep it away from other plants.

The Greeks called fennel 'marathon' meaning to grow thin. Whether this had anything to do with running 26 miles or was so called because of its disgestive qualities, I am not sure. According to Greek legend, Prometheus stole a spark from the fire on Mount Olympus and hid it in the stalk of a fennel. It was revered by the Romans as a strength-giving herb, and was also considered good for the eyes, and is still used today as an eyewash for sore and tired eyes.

Sow seed or divide the roots of an established plant in the spring. Do not confuse with Florence fennel, which is a vegetable grown for its bulbous root. Common fennel is useful as a good anise flavouring for fish dishes and for soups and stews. The leaves can also be used raw in salads.

Related species are *Foeniculum vulgare purpureum*, known as bronze fennel, and *F. vulgare*, Florence fennel, which is an annual cultivated for its succulent root.

Fragaria vesca

Alpine Strawbery

Family: Rosaceae
Other names: Steawberie, strewbridge, *fraise du bois*
Life: Hardy perennial

A delicate-leafed spreader that makes a wonderful border plant, sending out runners to invade the territory all around it. Alpine strawberry thrives in woodland and semi-shade, producing tiny, but delicious tasting red fruits. Originally introduced into Europe from Virginia it has been developed by cross-fertilisation into the large fleshy fruit that is today's strawberry. Its name derives from the Old English 'strewbridge', suggesting its ability to strew itself over the ground. John Gerard said of it that 'the distilled water drunke with white wine is good against the passion of the hart, reviving the spirits, and maketh the heart merrie.' It is still considered by medical herbalists to be a good laxative, diuretic and astringent. Linnaeus used its berries as a cure for rheumatic gout. Traditionally, it was used for removing tartar from the teeth, and the juice was also supposed to remove discolouration.

Runners can be divided early in the growing season. The leaves die back in the autumn, but the plant returns doubly revived in the spring. It is a good companion plant to borage, growing well in its natural shade.

Reputedly, wild strawberry is a great culinary favourite in France, where the fruit is picked in the early autumn and served in Parisian restaurants as a delicacy with *crême d'Isigny*. Strawberries have always been highly thought of in Britain too. Here is Thomas Tusser, writing in 1568: 'Wife unto the garden and set me a plot/With strawberry rootes of the best to be got.'

The related species *Fragaria moschata*, is known as musk strawberry. This is a wild plant with larger flowers. Also, *F. virginiana*, the original wild American strawberry, was much used by the North American Indians in herbal medicine.

Galium odoratum

Woodruff

Family: Rubiaceae
Other names: Sweet Woodruff, *muge-de-boys*
Life: Perennial

Woodruff is a late spring-flowering, shade-loving herb that, as its name implies, grows in woodland. The dark green leaves encircle the square stems at even intervals, and resemble Elizabethan ruffs. When brought into the house and dried, it has the intoxicating scent of new-mown hay. As a result it was a strewing herb, and was also used to stuff mattresses and to perfume bed linen. In Germany it is steeped in white wine and made into a May Day drink known as *Maibowle*.

Woodruff can be divided in the spring when it first appears after the winter, and roots can be taken for most of the year. This herb is a marvellous spreading plant and seems to double its size each year. In spring the tiny white flowers appear to float above the ruffs, and they look wonderful en masse. Medicinally, woodruff is a favourite with gypsies, who make it into a tea. It has been used to increase milk flow in young mothers, and also has a nervine effect. Woodruff has proved to be helpful in the treatment of such diverse conditions as constipation, forgetfulness, jaundice and hysteria, and for reducing feverishness. However, this is not a herb to take too much of, and a decent interval between treatments is advised.

John Gerard, in *The Herball* (1597), informs us that: 'Hanged up in houses, it doth very well attemper the aire, coole and make fresh the place to the delight and comfort of such as are therein.'

Related species include *Galium verum*, known as 'lady's bedstraw', which is a much taller, more ragged herb with yellow flowers, and *Asperula tinctoria*, known as 'dyer's woodruff'. Both of these have been used for dyeing.

Hypericum perforatum

St John's Wort

Family: Clusiaceae/Guttiferae
Other names: Herb John, balm of warriors' wounds, hundred holes, touch-and-heal, terrestrial sun
Life: Perennial

St John's wort was a favourite wound-healing herb at the time of the Crusades, but its reputation goes back even further, to Dioscorides, who in the 1st century AD compiled De Materia medica detailing the sources and uses of plants.

When held up to the light you can see the oil glands in the plant's leaves, which resemble tiny holes, or perforations. The flowers are yellow, but turn the colour of blood when crushed, and, if placed in a jar with a little olive oil in full sun will yield a dark red oil. This oil is very effective against burns and wounds.

The flowers and leaves of St John's wort have been used to treat anxiety, depression and excitability, and the herb has been referred to as the 'arnica of the nervous system'.

St John's wort will grow well in shady places and along ditches and banks. You can divide its roots in the spring or sow seeds in seed trays. Flowers were traditionally gathered on St John's Day, which falls on 24 June. This herb has many legends attached to it. It was thought of as a 'magic' herb because of its healing properties. The name *hypericum* means 'over an apparition', from the belief that it drives away evil spirits. It was regarded as a protective herb against fire and lightning. Another belief was that if a childless wife went naked to pick the flowers she would conceive within the year. Should you step on St John's wort on the Isle of Wight you would be carried off on a fairy horse, and not returned until morning.

There are a number of species in the hypericum family, but the only one closely related to St John's wort is *H. androsaemum*. Like *H. perforatum* it is a celebrated wound herb, but is larger and has black berries in autumn.

Hyssopus officinalis

Hyssop

Family: Labiatae
Other names: sope, hissop, hysope
Life: Perennial

It is well worth the wait for hyssop flowers to appear in mid to late summer. The deep blue whorls on tall, fragrant spikes are much loved by bees. Grown in large groups hyssop has a heady effect on the senses. It makes a good hedging plant but often at the expense of the flowers. I prefer to grow the smaller 'rock hyssop' for this purpose. You can allow it to grow to its full height of about 30cm/12in, having planted it no more than 20cm/8in apart. The flowers are even deeper in colour than those of the ordinary hyssop.

It has been suggested that this dwarf form, *Hyssopus aristatus*, could be the hyssop referred to in the bible. Psalm 51 verse 7 reads: 'Purge me with Hyssop, and I shall be clean.' And Sir John Harrington, in The Englishman's Doctor (1607) informs us that: 'Cleante Hyssop is an herbe to purge and clense/Raw flegmes, and hurtful humours from the brest...'

One drawback to cultivating hyssop, which likes a dry, well-drained soil with full sun, is that it tends to go woody and needs replacing every four years. But it produces plenty of seed, which is easy to harvest, and cuttings can be taken before flowering in the summer.

There is a bitter constituent in hyssop called 'marrubin', which gives it its expectorant qualities. Taken as a tisane it can be beneficial in treating upper respiratory infections and chest complaints. Sprinkled on meats it helps to break down the fat. It is not as popular today as a culinary herb, but it remains an important ingredient in a famous liqueur, chartreuse.

Of the pink and white forms of hyssop I find that the white form grows better for me. But that may depend on the growing conditions, such as the local climate and its situation in the garden.

Laurus nobilis

Bay

Family: Lauraceae
Other names: Sweet bay, noble laurel, daphne, Roman laurel
Life: Perennial

Anyone who has tasted the leaf fom the bay tree in Provence will tell you of its significant flavour. The warm sun seems to linger within its volatile oils imparting a spicy taste which conjures up images of slopes covered in olive trees, sweet mimosa and vines. The overall feeling of bay is that of goodness, and although it is native to the Mediterranean it will prosper well in northern Europe too. The trees can grow to a height of 12m/40ft; confined to more manageable proportions they can be trimmed into pyramid or ball shapes. At my first nursery I trimmed a 4 m-/13ft-high specimen into an umbrella shape and it provided perfect shade for the woodruff growing under it.

A sheltered site is important and you have to be patient in the early years, as laurel grows slowly. A position near the house provides comfort for tree and owner alike. Bay is a herb associated with the Greek god Apollo and with glory. Wreaths have crowned many victorious heads since the days of the Romans. The title 'poet laureate' derives from this use. The herb is said to ward off evil and as such was used for Christmas decoration. It is an evergreen and should not be pruned until early summer. In the event of severe damage by wind or frost, some success has been achieved in cutting the tree right down to the ground in order to help it regenerate.

To dry the leaves, lightly press them under a board and keep out of the sun in order to preserve the essential oils. Store in glass jars rather than bags.

CAUTION: The variety *Prunus laurocerasus* (cherry laurel) popularly known as 'laurel' is highly poisonous and should not be confused with this beautiful culinary plant.

Lavandula angustifolia

Lavender

Family: Labiatae
Other names: English lavender, true lavender
Life: Perennial

There are many varieties of lavender, but the one with the strongest scent and the most volatile oils is the English lavender, cultivated extensively in Norfolk, England, and famously in the Provence region of France. There it is known as 'French lavender' a name given in this country to *Lavandula stoechas*, a smaller form with ornamental purple bracts rather than the whorls on longer stems characteristic of *L. angustifolia*.

Lavender flowers throughout the summer and should be harvested on a dry day soon after the sun has dried the early morning dew off the leaves. It is much loved of bees and for this and other reasons no garden should be without a bush of lavender. It can be clipped into a hedge, but care should be taken not to cut back into old wood.

There are two schools of thought about when to prune lavender, spring or autumn. I prefer to cut off all the spikes in early autumn and then wait until the new spring growth is showing before shaping the bush. This will also give the bush a chance to build up its strength for the new year. Early autumn, however, is a good time to take hardwood cuttings. Growing from seed takes a long time.

Lavender derives its name from *lavare*, which is Latin for 'wash'. Thought of even today as a herb for the bath it has great cleansing properties. Lavender water makes a refreshing face wash, and a bowl of lavender flowers sweetens a room when disturbed by the fingers. Spikes of lavender used to be burned in the fireplace to fumigate a sick room.

Of the many varieties, I particularly like 'Hidcote', a smaller bush with deep blue flowers, or 'Munstead Dwarf', ideal as a low border. *L. stoechas* is well worth growing for its scent and for its unusual, spikey flowers.

Levisticum officinale

Lovage

Family: Umbelliferae
Other names: Love parsley, old English lovage, bishop's weed, king's cumin
Life: Perennial

Mrs C F Leyel, celebrated champion of herbal medicine in the 1940s, lists lovage as a 'herb to control pain'. This referred to its traditional use in relieving rheumatic pain. Thought of today more as a culinary herb, lovage has a long history, beginning with its introduction into Europe from India. It was reputed to have aphrodisiac properties and was worn as a love charm in Eastern Europe. A monastic herb in the Middle Ages, it has been suggested that lovage was used to give protection against the plague.

I grow lovage at the back of borders as it can grow as high as 2m/6ft. It is quite striking when it comes into flower during mid-summer, with umbrella-shaped yellow flowers on long stems. The leaves are bright green and broad in shape. Because of its size and large rootstock it is advisable to plant it in a rich, deep, well-drained soil, giving the roots a chance to seek water. One plant will supply a family's needs for the year, by cutting back several times during the summer months. It is easily increased by root division in the autumn or very early spring. The soil around young plants should be kept moist. Seeds can be sown under glass in the spring.

The leaves are used to flavour soups, or to make into a soup on their own. They are also used to flavour casseroles and any sauce that needs a light celery flavour. The stems can be candied, like angelica. The large leaves also make useful additions to flower arrangements.

Although medical herbalists use lovage as a warming digestive tonic and to treat menstrual problems, it has been shown to have an adverse effect on diseased kidneys. It should also be avoided during pregnancy.

Lippia citriodora

Lemon Verbena

Family: Verbenaceae
Other names: Herb Luisa, Spanish thyme, *Aloysia triphylla*, lemon-scented verbena.
Life: Perennial

Lemon verbena is native to Chile. As a result it needs a very warm sheltered climate in order to survive cold winter months. It is best grown in a large container and brought in at the first sign of frost. It is the most fragrant of all the lemon scents in the garden and therefore makes a tasty addition to summer desserts and drinks. The sedative effect of a tea infused from the leaves has made it a most popular calming tisane to take at night or after meals.

Lemon verbena forms quite a tall shrub that can be trained against a wall or grown as a corner feature in a conservatory. The leaves are pointed, long and narrow. It will grow well in a light, well-cultivated soil and requires very little attention except in the late autumn, when a mulch can be beneficial in protecting its roots for the winter. Harvest and dry the leaves at the time of flowering and store in airtight jars. The leaves will retain their flavour well. It has been used in finger bowls and the oil extracted from the herb is used for making soaps and perfume.

Lemon verbena is often confused with *Verbena officinalis,* called 'vervain' in some countries. The confusion arises from the fact that lemon verbena is called 'verveine' in France; it is used to relieve nausea, flatulence and dyspepsia.

The olfactory memory in many children brought up by Victorian nannies was that of lemon verbena, which they associated with their mothers, who would place a leaf of the herb between the breasts to act as a natural deodorant when wearing a ball-gown. When the rarely-seen mother went to the nursery to kiss the chilren before leaveing for the evening, the all-pervading scent filled the air long after her departure.

Melissa officinalis

Lemon Balm

Family: Labiatae
Other names: Bee balm, melissa, sweet balm
Life: Perennial

John Hussey of Sydenham breakfasted every morning for 50 years on lemon balm tea sweetened with honey. He died at the ripe old age of 116. Is it hardly surprising that lemon balm is classed as a 'long life' herb? Melissa, as it is often called (meaning 'bee' in Greek), is a delightful lemon-scented member of the mint family and is one of the easiest herbs to grow. It self-seeds freely and will root from the smallest piece. As a result it can be quite invasive and needs to be kept in check.

The best way is to cut it hard back before it gets a chance to flower in mid-summer. You can clip it into ball shapes at about this time too. The leaves are oval-shaped and finely toothed with a strong scent of lemon. Because of this they make wonderful additions to salads and summer drinks. In the 17th century, in the time of William Shakespeare, lemon balm was much in favour as a herb for polishing furniture.

The Carmelite nuns created an elixir tonic called Carmelite Water using brandy, nutmegs and angelica root with lemon rind and the leaves of lemon balm. You can use the leaves for summer drinks, salads and desserts. The fresh leaves make a refreshing tisane. To make a sleep-inducing tea, infuse equal parts of chamomile flowers, lemon balm and St John's wort.

Balm oil and hot water infusions have been used externally to treat shingles. As it induces sweating it makes a very useful treatment for colds and flu. It also reduces blood pressure.

Beekeepers have grown lemon balm near hives for generations because of its abundant nectar, and there is an old theory that a hive rubbed inside with the leaves will never lose its bees.

Mentha

Mint

Family: Labiatae
Other names: Mynts, mintes, myntes
Life: Perennial

'If any man can name the full list of all the kinds of mint, he must know how many sparks Vulcan sees fly into the air from his vast furnace benath Etna.' So wrote Walafrid Strabo in AD 840. Times do not change, and it is just as difficult to differentiate between various mints today as it was in the time of Walafrid Strabo. When I laid out my first nursery garden I placed four mints in close proximity to each other. Although they were divided by roof slates their roots managed to become entangled and some very strange looking mint plants developed.

All mints are among the easiest herbs to grow and the most difficult to control. The moment they are planted they send out roots in all directions. Try to contain them and you end up with a very unhappy prisoner that needs dividing and replanting every year. Because there are so many variations on a theme I will list just four representative of the group..

Round-leafed mint, *Mentha rotundifolia,* and its varieties, also known as apple mint, Bowles mint, pineapple mint or variegated apple mint, is the most sweetly-scented of the mint family. Spearmint, *Mentha spicata*, also known as garden mint, mackerel mint, lamb mint, provides constant argument as to whether this is the best mint to put with potatoes or not. Peppermint, *Mentha piperita,* also known as brandy mint, is the mint most used by medicinal herbalists. It has dark, almost purple leaves.

Pennyroyal, *Mentha pulegium*, also known as pudding grass, lurk-in-the ditch, is a prostrate form which does well in damp shade. It likes being crushed and emits a strong smell. It is a powerful abortive and should never be given to pregnant women. The name *pulegium* comes from the Latin 'pulex', meaning flea, as it has the reputation of detering fleas. I use it as an ant repellent.

Monarda didyma

Bergamot

Family: Labiatae
Other names: Bee balm, Oswego tea, scarlet monarda
Life: Perennial

Bergamot was cultivated extensively by the Oswego Indians of North America. This particular variety is the wild bergamot, *Monarda fistulosa*, which was introduced into Europe in 1656. The leaves and flowers were used to make Oswego tea, a soothing, relaxing tisane with the fragrance of oranges. Confusingly, the flavouring for Earl Grey tea is from the Spanish bergamot orange tree, and although we have taken the name 'bergamot' from that species it is as well to refer to this herb by its botanical name.

The plant we cultivate most often in our gardens today is a species related to the wild bergamot and was introduced in 1752. This is *Monarda didyma* and is most popular with bees, which makes it a must for any garden. The square stems, which grow to a height of 90cm/39in, have ovate, toothed leaves with large whorls of red flowers which are particularly attractive to bees. Bergamot prefers to grow in light shade with moist soil; if the soil is not well drained enough the plant tends to be smaller and prone to mildew. The best form of propagation is by root division, although seeds can be sown in the spring.

Medicinally, bergamot has been used to relieve flatulence, nausea and painful period pains. There are many varieties of bergamot, offering crimson purple, white or pink flowers. My favourite is 'Croftway Pink'.

The national collection of *Monarda* species is housed at Leeds Castle in Kent, England, under the stewardship of the head gardener Mr Maurice Bristow, who is, in my opinion, one of the kindest experts you are ever likely to meet.

Myrrhis odorata

Sweet Cicely

Family: Umbelliferae
Other names: Wild chervil, sweet ciss, anise fern, shepherd's needle
Life: Perennial

Sweet Cicely is a bushy, decorative herb with fern-like leaves. It grows to a height of 2m/6ft and spreads to 1m/39in, making it a good backdrop plant to any border. It blends well with more solid-looking, upright plants such as foxglove or evening primrose.

The stem is thick and ridged and the flowers, appearing in late spring or early summer, are creamy white. It has a sweet, anise scent and is much loved by the bees.

The seeds should be sown in the autumn in order to germinate in frosty ground. If you do not want to plant in situ you can sow seeds in trays left outside. It has a long thick taproot, so a well cultivated rich soil helps it to grow.

Roots can be divided in spring or autumn. It may be necessary to check for self-sown seedlings as it can be quite invasive. The seeds are dark brown and grow about 5cm/1in long.

Sweet Cicely makes a useful sugar substitute for people with diabetes, and a flavourful addition to fruit salads. It has always been considered a safe herb, and can be used freely without any fear of side effects. Traditionally it was used as a tonic for young girls during the transition from puberty to womanhood. It can be made into a warming tisane, being a gentle stimulant for the stomach.

Native Americans used the whole plant, and particularly the seeds and root, in their diet. The root has also been used as a lure for horses in order to catch them.

The French like to stuff their pillows with the dried herb.

Myrtus communis

Myrtle

Family: Myrtaceae
Other names: Myrte, mirto
Life: Perennial

Myrtle is a herb that is dedicated to the protection of virgins, symbolising purity and fertility. In European countries it is often woven into a bridal wreath. There was a tradition in Tuscany of lovers giving each other a love token of myrtle. If it was not presented at each meeting the engagement was effectively ended.

Legend has it that Aphrodite was turned into a myrtle tree to disguise her from the Satyrs when she became lost in a wood. In ancient Egypt it was considered to be a powerful medicine, and Pliny claimed that the Egyptian myrtle had the most powerful scent of all. A similar claim about Greek myrtle was made some 300 years earlier by Theophrastus. It is no wonder. In a hot climate the perfume must be wonderful.

Myrtle prefers a fertile soil in full sun, and in this country, grows best in a conservatory where it can be trained against a wall. The best time to do this is after flowering, in late summer. The flowers, set off by the dark, shiny green leaves, are like the flowers of a wild rose, white or blush-pink, and give way to dark berries. The leaves are a favourite in game dishes. It is not much used in medicine these days but was traditionally used for pains of the chest and for people suffering from consumption. A toilet water, known as angel water, *eau d'ange*, can be made from myrtle, and I have recently come across a hair ointment made by Ancient Egyptians that used a red mineral, myrtle, gazelle dung and hippopotamus fat – who's going to run their fingers through that hair?

The variegated form *M. communis* 'Variegata' has cream blotches on the leaves, which sometimes extend to the leaf margins and form a very delicate-looking border.

All in all, this is a very feminine herb.

Nepeta cataria

Catnip

Family: Labiatae
Other names: Nep, cat-nep, nepte
Life: Perennial

'If you set it, the cats will eat it,
If you sow it, the cats don't know it'.
Old English saying

Having witnessed the delight with which my cats roll about in catnip it is easy to understand John Gerard's description in *The Herball*. He says: 'The later Herbarists doe call it Herba Cattaria, because cats are very much delighted herewith for the smell of it is so pleasant unto them, that they rub themselves upon it, and wallow or tumble in it, and also feed on the branches and leaves very greedily.' It has been suggested by some that it has an aphrodisiac effect on cats. There is a rather charming suggestion in Agnus Castus in the 14th century, saying, 'The vertu of this herbs is as if a cat ete thereof it schal conseywyn and brynge forth kytlngis anon.'

If you are not a cat lover this is a herb to avoid in your garden. It is, however, a pretty plant resembling lemon balm with hairy soft leaves, light grey and heart shaped. The white flowers are borne on soft spikes.

Catnip is best propagated by root division in the spring, or you can take cuttings in the summer. These two methods do seem to produce a plant more attractive to my cats. A favourite toy you can make for your cat is a catnip-mouse, using the dried leaves of the plant and sowing them into a felt cover.

Medicinally, catnip is a very useful herb for children. Its gentle action in soothing the effects of colds and flu and in relaxing the nervous system make it a useful addition to the first aid cupboard.

Other varieties include *Nepeta mussinii*, the common garden catmint, and the smaller *Nepeta faassenii*, both of which make excellent blue-flowering border plants.

Ocimum basilicum

Basil

Family: Labiatae
Other names: Sweet basil, sweet genovese
Life: Annual

In recent years basil has become an extremely popular herb, probably as a result of advances in greenhouse techniques. It is native to India and requires a hot humid atmosphere in order to thrive. This does not mean to say it cannot be grown outside in temperate climates. Provided it is sheltered from winds and given plenty of light in a rich, well drained soil it will flourish, although not in the luxuriant way of the pampered indoor plant.

I have found it to be a most demanding herb that rewards you well if used regularly and watered morning, noon and early evening in full sun. Do not water at night as it hates to go to bed with its feet wet, and do not be tempted to take too much from it too soon. I have found that the seed germinates quickly when sown in early summer and it will grow on well if transferred to small pots at the four-leaf stage. The seeds are large enough to sow singly in plug trays; they form a strong root system.

Basil is best torn with the fingers, as tearing imparts a better flavour. Preserved in olive oil with the addition of a little coarse salt, it will provide you with a winter reminder of hot summer days. It is a good idea to keep it apart from rue in the garden. Pinch out the flower heads as soon as they appear and cut hard back in the autumn.

Sweet basil is the most widely used variety and the easiest to cultivate. Others to try are the dwarf form of bush or Greek basil, and the dark opal purple form. Sacred basil (*Ocimum sanctum*), known as 'tulsi' in India, is very highly scented.

It is an insect repellent and excellent tisane when combined with rosemary (one part basil to two parts rosemary) to combat the effects of tiredness.

Oenothera biennis

Evening Primrose

Family: Onagraceae
Other names: Tree primrose, evening star, king's cure-all
Life: Biennial

In recent years it came as some surprise to the scientific world that this garden 'escape' plant should have kept its secrets for so long. The essential oils of this strikingly beautiful herb were found to contain large quantities of a substance called gammalinoleic acid. Research, which is still continuing, has shown that this substance is effective in the treatment of blood clotting, pre-menstrual tension (PMT), arthritis, eczema, liver damage caused by alcohol abuse and countless other benefits to our well-being.

In the garden evening primrose makes a beautiful backdrop to a border, particularly if there is a wall or wattle fence behind it. The plant grows to a height of anything up to 1.5m/5ft with yellow trumpet-shaped flowers starting from the top of the plant in mid to late summer. The flowers look well in the evenings, giving rise to the common name; the individual flowers survive only for a day but others are produced further down the stems. Seed capsules develop when the flowers fade, guaranteeing plants for the next season.

Evening primrose will grow in most soils, providing there is good drainage, and prefers sun although it is quite happy in light shade too. Seeds should be sown in early summer so that the young plantlets can be set out in autumn for flowering the following year.

The roots of evening primrose have been used as a vegetable and the flowers make a pretty ingredient for salads, a common usage in France.

Origanum majorana

Marjoram

Family: Labiatae
Other names: Sweet marjoram, amaracus, joy of the mountain
Life: Perennial

I have included oregano under this heading as it is of the same family. The name oregano comes from two Greek words meaning 'joy of the mountains', and this is a herb associated with happiness. It was planted on graves as a cheerful farewell and was given to couples in a wedding garland.

There are several varieties of marjoram, the most often seen being sweet marjoram - also known as knotted marjoram, pot marjoram, golden marjoram, gold-tipped marjoram - and the wild marjoram, known as oregano. All are perennial, although strictly speaking sweet marjoram is a tender perennial best grown annually each spring. They all prefer dry, fertile soil with plenty of hot sunshine.

Marjoram is a bushy, shrub-like plant with oval leaves on woody stems. The mounded cushions of pot marjoram, most striking in the golden marjoram, make useful shapes on higher and sloping ground, although they tend to fall away from the centre when in flower. The flowers of oregano grow in mauve clusters and have a heady, musty scent and are most attractive to bees. As a result oregano was a popular strewing herb and was used in nosegays, as well as being used to scour furniture. Marjoram has also been used in hair tonics and in snuff, and is reported to have a beneficial effect on the brain. Its culinary uses are for stuffings in sausages, meat and poultry, and flavouring for soups. I also like to add a few leaves to salads.

Traditionally, marjoram was used for flavouring beer, and it also has good digestive qualities. I like to use it in digestive tonics, steeped in wine. It is the bitter constituents of this herb which aid digestion and prepare the stomach before eating.

Petroselinum crispum

Parsley

Family: Umbelliferae
Other names: Parcely, persely, perslie
Life: Biennial

There are several superstitions attached to parsley, one being that the seed goes to the devil and back seven times before germinating. It does take a long time. But not that long. There are ways to speed up the process. One is to soak the seed overnight before sowing. The other is to pour boiling water on the seed in its drills. I prefer to let nature take its course, sow in plug trays placed in a cold greenhouse and check regularly for the little green hooks to appear. The mistake often made, and I have made it myself, is to allow too many stalks to a pot, or together in the ground. Thin to at least 30 cm/12in apart in a well cultivated soil and site where it can get some afternoon shade. It is a hungry plant and therefore needs feeding and watering well, the best time being late afternoon. Do not be tempted to denude it of leaf too soon in its development. Plants sown in spring will go to seed early the following year, so it is best sown again in late summer for a good crop next year.

Medicinally it is classed as a bitter aromatic. This points to it being a good herb for the digestion. It has been used in the treatment of cystitis, to strengthen the urinary tract and for flushing out toxins from the body. It is the next best source of iron after nettles, and is rich in vitamin C. A good restorative herb, but it should be avoided by pregnant women, although it is used to help the womb recover after birth. Parsley is also recommended as a kidney tonic.

It is well accepted as a garnish and makes a marvellous sauce. There is a plain-leafed form often called 'Italian' or 'French' parsley (*Petroselinum hortense*) which imparts a very strong flavour but is not so attractive as a garnish. A sprig of parsley really does sweeten the breath after eating garlic.

Rosa gallica officinalis

Rose

Family: Rosaceae
Other names: Apothecary rose
Life: Perennial

Rose oil, rose water, rose hip syrup, they all conjure up images of beauty and fragrance. The 'true' roses of herb gardens are the old roses, with pedigrees that date back to the Mogul Empire. These roses are blush-pink, red and soft white, with such delicate flowers growing on the sharpest of thorned stems. *Rosa gallica*, the 'Apothecary's' rose in Britain and some other countries, and 'Provence' rose in France, is the one most used in medicine. The dog rose, *Rosa canina,* is the most nutritious. It was given its name because of its reputed ability to cure rabies. The Damask rose, *Rosa gallica versicolor,* is the most popular for making pot-pourri. It is also known as *Rosa mundi*. Sadly, the flowering period of these old roses is short – a matter of three or four weeks in early summer. So it is best to consult an early rose specialist to mix in some of the newer Gallica introductions that have a longer flowering time. Rose petals can be gathered when dry and laid out on paper in an airy shady place and added to scented geranium leaves for a long lasting pot-pourri. All roses require full sun and a well manured soil in which to thrive. One great benefit of the old scented roses is that they need no more than a light prune after flowering, and they shape quite nicely, usually covering an area of about 1.2 sq m/4sq. feet.

The 'sweet eglantine' of Shakespeare's day is the 'sweet briar', smaller in leaf and flower and so called because of its sweet scent.

All the wild roses make good impenetrable hedges. Their hips, which are three times richer in vitamin C than an orange, and the scent of the flowers, are nature's gift to sweeten all the senses.

Rosmarinus officinalis

Rosemary

Family: Labiatae
Other names: Compass-weed, polar plant, *incensier* (Old French)
Life: Perennial

On 23 April, Shakespeare's birthday, the people of Stratford-upon-Avon carry sprigs of rosemary in procession through the streets. This follows an old tradition that rosemary keeps the memory green. Claudius refers to this in *Hamlet*, in his first speech of the play: 'Though yet of Hamlet our dear brother's death/The memory be green...' The belief was that if a sprig of rosemary was placed in the hands of the deceased it would sprout and create a fragrant bush covering the rotting corpse.

Rosemary is one of the universally great herbs and, in the upright form of *R. officinalis,* develops into a splendid strong and fragrant bush displaying light blue flowers – so beloved by bees – for many months of the year. Grow in a well-drained soil with plenty of grit to allow the roots to breathe. Cuttings can be taken from spring right through the year except at the height of summer. Use stems that are not in flower and place in moist sharp sand in a shady place or sow seeds in the spring. To really thrive, rosemary needs full sun and a dry soil, well sheltered, although the best bush I ever had was on a windswept allotment.

Trim back soon after planting and take from it on a regular basis and it will reward you with strong new shoots and a healthy, oily leaf. Just to rub the branches of rosemary makes you feel good. Make it into a tisane to lift the spirits. Bring a flowering stem into the home to energise you. It derives its name from two words, 'ros' meaning 'dew' and 'marinus' meaning 'sea', probably because of its natural habitat along the Mediterranean coasts.

There are many types of rosemary, from the prostrate *R. officinalis prostrata*, to the delicate flowered 'Frimley Blue', and the sturdy 'Miss Jessopp's Upright'.

Rumex acetosa

Sorrel

Family: Polygonaceae
Other names: Green sauce, sour suds, cuckoo sorrow
Life: Perennial

The juicy stems and leaves of garden sorrel are the prime ingredients in *soupe aux herbes*, a favourite French dish. The leaves are high in oxalic acid, which imparts a crisp, sharp taste that made this a herb reputed among country folk to quench the thirst. It likes moist, rich soil and will tolerate partial shade. Arrow-shaped, lush green leaves quickly form into large clumps developing tall flower stems of reddish-brown that grow to a height of 1m/3ft. Cut the leaves on a regular basis as this helps to increase the crop.

The vitamin C content of sorrel made it a traditional remedy for scurvy. Today it is best avoided by people who suffer from gout, or kidney stones, as the crystals created by the oxalic acid can activate these symptoms.

The low-growing buckler leaf sorrel, also known as French sorrel, is lower in oxalic acid but very sharp in taste. The leaves are shield-shaped and abundant, and have small flowering stems. These should be cut off as soon as they appear to encourage more leaf growth. Buckler leaf sorrel makes a splendid addition to salads and is very refreshing to take on hot days in the garden.

Other related species of sorrel include broad-leaf sorrel and the silver form of buckler leaf called 'Silver Shield Leaf'. The broad leaf is a favourite of my wife's, as it puts out very little in the way of flower and grows in thick clumps. It is also a smaller variety than the common garden sorrel and is ideal for a small area. The Hopkinsons of Hollington Nurseries have developed a broad-leaf variety from rootstock which does not produce seed and grows to a height of only 30cm/12in. It is called 'Hollington Broad Leaf' and produces a very tender green leaf.

Ruta graveolens

Rue

Family: Rutaceae
Other names: Herb of grace, herby-grass, garden rue
Life: Perennial

In recent years, Rue has become the *bête noire* of the herb garden. Members of the rue family can cause phototoxic reactions. This means that when exposed to direct sunlight the plant secretes a volatile oil which, in some people, can cause burns and blisters on the skin. Because of this it is at the top of the list of 'hazardous' plants, and should not be planted where children play or where people might be bathing. Whether or not rue has only recently developed this dangerous side to its nature, the traditional view of this most decorative herb is of healing and holiness.

Mithridates the Great, King of Pontus, used rue as the main ingredient in an antidote to poison. It was regarded as a protection against evil, and Catholic priests were supposed to have used rue as an aspergillum to anoint the congregation with holy water. This gave it the lovelyname 'herb of grace'. In the early 18th century it was used in the infamous 'vinegar of the four thieves' and judges would place a sprig of rue on the bench between them and the defendant to protect them from 'gaol fever'. It is still carried, symbolically, by judges to this day on processions to the assizes. The blue-grey, club-shaped leaves were granted as a chaplet for the heraldic device of the first duke of Saxony in 1181. This symbol later became the model for the suit of clubs in playing cards. Rue will grow to a height of 1m/30in, forming a semi-evergreen woody shrub. The flowers are bright yellow and are carried in clusters on grey-green stems.

You should keep rue well away from basil: they dislike each other.

Caution: Do not use for self-medication; rather, consult a qualified medical herbalist.

Salvia officinalis

Sage

Family: Labiatae
Other names: Sawge, salgia, salvia, salvatrix
Life: Perennial

The botanical name for sage derives from the Latin 'salvere' meaning 'to save'. In the 16th century it acquired a reputation for promoting long life. Thomas Coghan, in his *Haven of Health* recorded, 'As I myselfe have knowen a man of 80 yeares and upwarde, who for his breakfast in summer used to eate 6 or 7 Sage leaves minced small with a little salt...by which means he preserves himselfe long in a healthfull state.' Before this time it was recognised as one of nature's great 'cure-alls'. An old Arabian proverb asks, 'How can a man die who has sage in his garden?' The Chinese were keen to give the Dutch traders three times the quantity of tea in exchange for sage leaf. In France it was looked upon as a grief herb, probably for the relief it gives to spasms in the chest region. This seems to have reached England in the 17th century when the famous diarist, Samuel Pepys, recorded seeing, 'Between Gosport and Southampton...a little churchyard where it was customary to sow all the graves with Sage.' In the war-torn coastal regions of former Yugoslavia, sage has long been a part of a thriving industry producing sage honey. In the garden the soft grey-green leaves of the common sage mix well with the dark purple leaves of red sage (*Salvia purpurea*) and variegated forms, such as 'Icterina', which are less hardy.

It grows best in full sun, in a well-drained soil. Prune back to young shoots in late spring and take cuttings to root in sharp sand, or layer bushes in autumn. Old woody bushes can be mounded up to produce new shoots in spring. Do not be disheartened by sage's straggly appearance in winter, as it will revive in the spring, when you can remove the tips to encourage new growth below.

Sanguisorba minor

Salad Burnet

Family: Rosaceae
Other names: *Pimpinella sanguisorba*, burnet saxifrage, lesser burnet.
Life: Perennial

This wild, unruly herb will give you sustained growth throughout the year. An easy plant to grow, it reaches a height of 40cm/15in, with small pinnate leaves having serrated edges. Of these, William Turner wrote in 1551: 'It has two little leaves like unto the wings of birdes, standing out as the bird setteth her wings when she intendeth to flye. Ye Dutchmen call it Hergottes Berdlen, that is "God's little birds", because of the colour that it hath in the top.'

The rosy-coloured, globular flower heads should be cut off if you want to produce plenty of leaf. On their own the leaves do not seem to taste much, but once put into a salad or wine drink they taste of chestnut mixed with cucumber. Salad burnet makes a useful substitute herb in the winter, if you want to use fresh leaves. It is a very good herb to include in windowboxes, as it fills out well providing all round interest. Keep it trimmed otherwise it gets to look a bit straggly and loses its charm. It will grow in most places in full sun or part shade and can be sown from seed in spring. If allowed to flower it will self-seed freely.

Salad burnet grows in the wild all over central Europe and along the North African coast. It will be found in woodlands, and fields on dry chalk.

Related species include *Sanguisorba officinalis,* known as great burnet, which has dark green leaves and red flowers and grows to 1m/39in in height. Other large forms include *S. obtusa* and *S. tenuifolia,* both of which grow to a height of 1.5m/5ft. The leaves of all varieties are edible, although salad burnet has the best flavour.

Traditionally, it used as a wound healer, soldiers having used it after battle to staunch the bleeding.

Santolina chamaecyparissus

Cotton Lavender

Family: Compositae
Other names: Lavender cotton, santolina
Life: Perennial

The branched silver-grey, coral-like stems of santolina make it a most decorative feature for any border edge. I like to mix it with the dark green variety, *Rosmarinifolia viridis* and clip the plants into flat and ball shapes.

John Parkinson sang the praises of cotton lavender as an edging plant as early as 1629. 'It is planted in Gardens to border knots with, for which it will abide to be cut into what forme you think best, for it groweth thick and bushy'.

Provided you cut santolina hard back in the spring to the new growth showing at the base of each stem, then, as John Parkinson suggests, you will be rewarded with bushy plants, ideal for low hedging. The tiny yellow button flowers are particularly striking, forming a heavily scented carpet of flower above the woody stems. The smell is not to everyone's liking, being pungent and rather heady. If the flower heads are removed the bushy growth is stronger and can be shaped.

To propagate, take cuttings in spring or autumn and set them in sharp sand. Like rosemary, the plant can be layered. It is a 'dry' herb that prefers a light soil which drains well, and it needs full sun. Traditionally it has been used as a vermifuge (used to expel intestinal worms) and moth repellent, and as a tisane, but it has no culinary use.

Other varieties include *S. chamaecyparissus* 'Nana' a more compact fom growing only 30cm/12in in height with coarse silver foliage and yellow flowers; Santolina 'Lemon Queen', which has softer creamy yellow flowers and a heavy scent 'Lambrook Silver' and another *S. viridis* form called 'Primrose Gem'. Sometimes *S. viridis* is listed as *S. rosmarinifolia*.

Satureia hortensis/S. montana

Savory

Family: Labiatae
Other names: Bean herb
Life: *S. hortensis,* annual; *S. montana,* perennial

Winter savory (*S. montana*) makes a sweet scented edging that is a delight to brush against. In Roman times it was considered to be an aphrodisiac, deriving its name from the satyrs. In Germany summer and winter savories were called *Bohnenkraut*, meaning 'bean herb', and they do indeed make a worthy addition to any bean dish. They have a similar appearance to thyme, but are more branched, with small pink or white flowers. The summer savory (*S. hortensis*) is an annual and should be sown in situ in early spring. The seeds take a long time to germinate but will produce plants for cutting by midsummer. The soil needs to be in full sun and quite rich. Thin out the seedlings to 15cm/6in.

Summer savory has a peppery taste and should be used sparingly. It is taller than winter savory, growing to a height of 45cm/18in, and tends to become rather straggly. Cut it two or three times during the growing season. It is a great favourite with bees, and the leaf is said to give relief from their sting.

Summer savory is used commercially to flavour salami. Both savories have been used as moth repellents in a similar way to southernwood, placing the stems between the garments. For good strong growth, it is best to cut winter savory hard back in early spring. Although it looks dreadful for three or four weeks it benefits greatly from this cutting and produces strongly favoured leaves as a result. Most cooks prefer the summer savory, but for my part I prefer the winter savory for its scent and for its usefulness as a fragrant, low-growing edging herb.

Symphytum officinale

Comfrey

Family: Boraginaceae
Other names: Knitbone, boneset, bruisewort, gumplant, solidago
Life: Perennial

Like all great healing herbs comfrey prefers light shade and will grow very well under trees. Ideally the soil should also be moist, but I have found it will grow quite happily in most soils. It propagates easily by root division, the smallest piece producing a new plant. For this reason it can be quite invasive and may need rooting out every three or four years. The whole plant grows to a height of 100cm/39in and is hairy and thick-stemmed. These hairs, as with borage, can be prickly to the touch and I would advise you to wear gloves when harvesting it. If you cut it down on a regular basis through the growing season, comfrey will yield plenty of leaf. It is a good compost herb, helping to break down the layers of waste material and adding rich nutrients to the heap. A liquid feed can be made from an infusion of the leaves. Organic growers find this a most useful plant for mulching, feeding and composting. Comfrey was introduced into England from Russia in 1871 by Henry Doubleday, who was the great pioneer of organic gardening.

The roots and leaves of comfrey can be used in herbal medicine. The presence of up to 0.8 per cent allantoin helps it to promote healing of fractured bones and bruises. It can be used as a poultice for varicose ulcers and as a compress for varicose veins. It has also proved helpful in the treatment of bronchial complaints.

There are two smaller forms of comfrey that I like to grow in the garden: *Symphytum grandiflorum*, a dwarf variety with pink and cream flowers, and *S. caucasicum* with striking blue flowers.

Some caution should be exercised in the use of comfrey as a tisane, as research has shown that it can have a carcinogenic effect on the liver.

Tanacetum parthenium

Feverfew

Family: Compositae
Other names: Featherfoil, flirtwort, bridesmaids' buttons
Life: Perennial

If ever there was a herb that fitted the description of a plant that 'grows like a weed', it's feverfew. For the many migraine sufferers who have found relief from eating the leaves it is just as well. This pungent, daisy-flowered garden escape demands a certain amount of respect. For although it can help to reduce the effect of migraine the leaf should be taken in very small quantities and rolled in a pellet of bread to avoid mouth ulcers. If you are unfortunate enough to suffer in this way then try using tincture of myrrh as a remedy. A tea made from feverfew leaves and flowers can sometimes help with depression.

There are other varieties of feverfew to grow in your borders. The golden form adds a splash of brightness, and the double-flowered variety also helps to offer new interest. All feverfew are very easy to grow, although I have found them susceptible to blackfly. A regular spray with Derris can usually eradicate this problem, and keep the plant safe to eat. It self-seeds freely, can be increased by root division in the spring and will grow quite well from cuttings taken in the autumn and early spring.

Feverfew has been used as an insect repellent. Traditionally, it was grown near buildings, in the belief that it would ward off evil spirits and disease. It is one of the first herbs to flower in the year and I use it as a plant to fill in gaps that have been left after the winter.

Related species are: *Tanacetum parthenium aureum*, known as golden feverfew, with striking yellow foliage and daisy white flowers. Also, a rarer double-flowering form, *T. parthenium* 'Double', which has white pom-pom flowers all summer. The leaf of both of these varieties can be used by migraine sufferers.

Tanacetum vulgare

Tansy

Family: Compositae
Other names: Bachelor's buttons
Life: Perennial

Tansy is a favourite gypsy herb and a common hedgerow plant that will grow in most soils. The flat-headed yellow flowers form a welded calyx resembling cloth buttons, and last all summer. The leaves are pungent and give off a camphor scent, which accounts for its use as an insect repellent. Housewives used to rub the meat with tansy leaves to keep off flies. In Greece it is called *'athansie'* meaning 'everlasting'. In legend, Gannymede used it to attain immortality, but it also had a darker use as a preservative for dead bodies. It is a very bitter herb and not to modern tastes, but until recently tansy cakes were eaten to end the Lenten fast. In the ancient school of medicine at Salerno, tansy was one of the six remedies recommended for palsy, although today medical herbalists would caution care in this treatment if the patient is of a nervous disposition. But, under qualified supervision, it is a most beneficial herb as a vermifuge, for expelling worms, for delayed periods and menstrual cramps and fevers. Externally it can be used for swellings, toothache, varicose veins, bruises, earache, styes and eye inflammation. Certainly it might have been viewed as a 'cure-all' at one time.

One word of caution: tansy, because of its ability to promote menstruation, should on no account be taken during pregnancy. This tends to contradict Nicholas Culpeper's belief, but even for the sake of tradition it is not a risk worth taking. It should also not be taken for any length of time.

Tansy is invasive and grows to at least 1m/39in, with a strong root system. As a companion plant it deters beetles, ants, aphids and cabbage moth. Grow it with cabbages, roses, raspberries and fruit trees and it will have a beneficial effect.

Teucrium chamaedrys

Wall Germander

Family: Labiatae
Other names: Common germander, hedge germander, *petit chêne*
Life: Perennial

Wall germander reaches a height of only 45cm/18in, with small green, oak-shaped, toothed leaves on branching woody stems. If it is clipped into shape before flowering it makes an ideal low border hedge, very similar to buxus, but infinitely cheaper. It also grows more quickly. If grown as a border plant the flowers appear for at least two months in summer; they are rose pink. Seeds can be sown in the spring, cuttings taken in summer and plants divided in autumn.

Wall germander grows well in a good loamy soil, with a small addition of grit or shingle. I have grown it as a low barrel-shaped hedge surrounding my front garden and although it only gets sun in the morning and early afternoon it has done very well. Wall germander was traditionally used for gout, Emperor Charles V having been a very grateful patient. Nicholas Culpeper recommended it for ulcers, tired eyes, pains in the side and cramps. He also suggests that it might have been effective for reviving the vital spirit. Its constitutents include an essential oil, and it has antiseptic, astringent and bitter tonic properties, among others. Today it is mostly used for the treatment of osteoarthritis.

Wall germander is native to southern and central Europe, where it grows in woodland, on dry, sunny banks, on rocks and walls. It was introduced to Britain as a medicinal herb and is now widely cultivated, although it can sometimes be found growing on old walls, where it has become naturalised. A related species, *Teucrium scorodonia*, or wood sage, is native to Britain. This has sage-like leaves with yellow flowers, and, as its name implies, grows well in shady places under trees.

Thymus vulgaris

Thyme

Family: Labiatae
Other names: Garden thyme, common thyme
Life: Perennial

Thyme originated in the Mediterranean regions, and is one of the most savoury of all the herbs growing in the garden. It is a woody, shrub-like herb with aromatic leaves and pale purple flowers, which are very attractive to bees. The word '*thumus*' is Greek for 'courage', and in the days of chivalry ladies would embroider a bee hovering over a sprig of thyme to present to their champions at the jousting tournaments. The association with magic and fairies was particularly noticeable during Shakespeare's time. In the Ashmolean Museum in Oxford there is a receipt (recipe) dated 1600 that includes thyme, which will 'Enable one to see the Fairies'.

Thyme grows very easily on stony, well drained soil in full sun. But it has the virtue of growing in any soil as long as it is not too moist. It takes well from cuttings in the summer, or you can divide plants in the spring. It is an evergreen, although it may need some protection in cold climates. A light prune in late autumn helps it to contain its strength. There are many varieties of upright and creeping thymes. Creeping thymes need careful cultivation and are not as frost hardy as the uprights, but they all make wonderful edgings and scented seats.

Medicinally, thyme has been associated with the treatment of depression. The volatile oil contains thymol, a most powerful antiseptic. This has been isolated and used in cough mixtures. It also helps to relieve flatulence and soothes the digestive system. An oil made from thyme has been used to treat shingles.

Like the sages, this strong herb gives so much of itself that every four years it is best to replace it; take cuttings from the second year on for this purpose

Urtica dioica

Stinging Nettle

Family: Urticaceae
Other names: Common nettle
Life: Perennial

Culpeper described stinging nettles as being, 'under the dominion of Mars', and so well known that, 'they may be found by feeling in the darkest night.' In the wild, stinging nettles are always found where the soil is fertile, even though it may appear to be a waste place. There is a story to illustrate this.

A blind man goes to investigate a field which he wishes to buy. On arriving at the field he asks the vendor if he might tether his donkey to the nearest clump of thistles. The vendor tells him there are no thistles. So the blind man asks if the donkey can be tied to the nearest bunch of nettles. The vendor tells him he can tie his donkey to wherever he likes as the field is full of stinging nettles. 'In that case,' says the blind man, 'I will buy your field.'

Stinging nettles invariably grow in clumps, having a similar invasive habit to mint. The leaf is very like the mint family, but they are covered in barbed hairs which contain formic acid and the resulting sting can be painful. Relief is often found from a companion plant growing nearby; the common dock. In spite of this, when cooked or placed in hot water they lose their sting and make a very good springtime tonic. The plant is a must in any medicinal garden, growing happily in sun or shade. It is a diuretic, diaphoretic (promotes sweating), expectorant and slyptic. It is rich in iron and stimulates the circulation. When the Romans came to Britain they brought a giant form of stinging nettle, *Urtica pilulifera*, with which they used to beat themselves to combat the cold of the north.

The stinging nettle is a most versatile plant: it is used to make thread for tablecloths and sheets, rope and paper. The leaves make a green dye and I often use them as a compost activator.

HERBS FOR SUN AND SHADE

Herbs that grow well in full sun

Basil
Bergamot (needs moist soil)
Borage
Chamomile
Coltsfoot
Cotton lavender (*santolina*)
Dill
Fennel
Hyssop
Lavender
Lady's mantle
Lemon verbena
Marigold (*calendula*)
Marjoram
Rue
Sage
Salad Burnet
Southernwood
Summer and winter savory
Tarragon
Thyme

Herbs that grow well in heavy shade

Deadly nightshade
Lily of the valley
Woodruff

Herbs that grow well in partial shade

Angelica
Jacob's ladder
Lady's mantle
Lungwort
Pennyroyal
Valerian
Wood sage

Herbs that grow well in some shade

Chives
Comfrey
Foxglove
Honeysuckle
Lady's bedstraw
Lemon balm
Mint
Parsley
Purslane
St John's wort

HERBS FOR COLOUR

Red

Apothecary rose
Bergamot
Clove pink
Pineapple sage

Blue

Borage
Flax
Jacob's ladder
Rosemary

Pink

Chives
Foxglove
Marjoram
Thyme 'Pink Chintz'
Thyme 'Annie Hall'
Wall germander

Purple

Basil 'Dark Opal'
Foxglove
Red orache
Red sage (leaf)
Thyme

Green/yellow

Dill
Fennel
Lady's bedstraw
Lady's mantle
Lovage
Rue (flowers)

Yellow

Elecampane
Evening primrose
St John's wort
Sunflower
Tansy

Orange

Nasturtium
Pot marigold

White/cream

Double-flowered chamomile
Feverfew
Garlic chives
Lily of the valley
Thyme 'Albus'
Valerian
Woodruff

Useful Addresses

Herb Nurseries

Cheshire Herbs
Fourfields
Forest Road
Little Budworth
near Tarporley
Cheshire CW6 9ES

Hollington Nurseries
Woolton Hill
Newbury
Berkshire RG15 9XT

Langley Boxwood Nursery
National Collection - Buxus
Rake
near Liss
Hampshire GU33 7JL

Jekka's Herb Farm
Rose Cottage
Shellards Lane
Alveston
Bristol BS12 2SY

Norfolk Lavender
Caley Mill
Heacham
KIngs Lynn
Norfolk PE31 7JE

Dried Herbs and Herb Products

Hambledon Herbs
Court Farm
Milverton
Somerset TA4 1NF

Neal's Yard Remedies
14-15 Neal's Yard
Covent Garden
London WC2 9DP

Associations and Societies

British Herbal Medicine Association
Lane House
Cowling
Keighley
West Yorkshire BD22 0LX

British Herb Society
134 Buckingham Palace Road
London SW1W 9SA

British Herb Trade Association
NFU Building
22 Long Acre
Covent Garden
London WC2E 9LY

Chelsea Physic Garden
Friends of the Chelsea Physic Garden
66 Royal Hospital Road
London SW3 4HS

Henry Doubleday Association
Ryton Gardens
Ryton-on-Dunsmore
Coventry CV8 3LG

National Institute of Medical Herbalists
148 Forest Road
Tunbridge Wells
Kent TN2 5EY

The Soil Association
86 Colston Street
Bristol BS1 5BB

The Tradescant Trust
Friends of the Museum of Garden History
Lambeth Palace Road
London SE1 7LB

Index